STRUM BOWING ETUDES

Viola

By Tracy Silverman

Music preparation by Mike Casteel
Layout by Austin Gray   www.entireworld.us
Painting and Drawings by Rachel Kice   www.rachelkice.com

All compositions Copyright © 2020 by Tracy Silverman
All rights reserved.
ISBN 978-1-7348145-0-7

No part of this book may be reproduced or transmitted in any form or by any means, electronic or mechanical, including photocopying, recording, or by any information storage and retrieval systems without written permission from the author or publisher, except for the inclusion of brief quotations in a review.

Published by Silverman Musical Enterprises, LLC
Nashville, TN
info@tracysilverman.com | www.tracysilverman.com | www.strumbowing.com

Table of Contents

Strum Etude 1: Step By Step	1
Strum Etude 2: Shades of the Ghost	6
Strum Etude 3: The Ghost of Grooves Past	10
Strum Etude 4: Groovin' the Ghost	12
Strum Etude 5: Deck the Halls with Placekeeper Notes	14
Strum Etude 6: The Groovon in the Dell	18
Strum Etude 7: Talk to the Hand	20
Strum Etude 8: Dancin' Fool	24
Strum Etude 9A: GPS (Groove Proficiency System)	26
Strum Etude 9B: The Strumming Waubonsies	30
Strum Etude 10: Down Down Down!	33
Strum Etude 11: Doin' the Strum	39
Strum Etude 12: Variations on a Groove	44
Strum Etude 13A: Triplets and the 12/8 Shuffle	47
Strum Etude 13B: Magic Sixes	51
Strum Etude 13C: Cross Currents	54
Strum Etude 13D: Groovin' the Seven	56
Strum Etude 13E: Smooth Fiver	59
Strum Etude 14: Chop 'Til You Drop	61
Strum Etude 15: Double-time It	66
Strum Etude 16: Hit It on the Back Beat	70
Strum Etude 17A: Groovin' the Chop	73
Strum Etude 17B: Swingin' the Chop	80
Strum Etude 18A: Changing Gears	82
Strum Etude 18B: Automatic Transmission–Swingin' the Chop 2	86
Strum Etude 19A: 3-D Barbecue	88
Strum Etude 19B: Compound Interest	93
Strum Etude 20: Groovin' on the Vertizontal	96
Strum Etude 21: Freestylin'—A Groove Jam	99

The Basics of
The Strum Bowing Method

Here are a few of the key concepts of Strum Bowing. There is a complete glossary at the end of the book.

Groovon:
The smallest particle of a rhythmic groove
- Just as atoms are made up of smaller elements, such as protons, neutrons and electrons, a beat is made up of what I call *Groovons*. These are the smallest particles of a groove—the fastest notes you hear in the song.

Subdivision:
1. *The act of dividing a pulse evenly into smaller increments. For instance, a quarter note can be divided into four sixteenth notes.*
2. *A fraction of a pulse, such as a sixteenth note.*
- You can subdivide time just as you can subdivide space. You can divide a pulse in music into smaller sub-pulses just as you can divide an inch into half and quarter inches. You can take a quarter note and divide it into two 8th notes or four 16th notes, and so on.

- This subdivision can show up on many different instruments. It could be the strumming of a guitar; the congas, bongos or the shaker in the percussion; a keyboard part; or a fast moving vocal part, as in a rap. If you want to be able to groove with a song, the first thing you have to do is find the Groovon.

Grid:
A consistent framework that helps keep rhythms evenly aligned; a rhythm ruler; a.k.a. The Groovon Grid.

- The consistent down/up motion of strumming creates a rhythmic grid. In the diagram above, each line of the grid represents a Groovon, a subdivision of the beat.

Groove:
A consistent subdivision of the pulse defined by a pattern of accented and ghosted notes.
- On strings, a groove is a pattern of down and up bows. Some of the strokes are accented, and some are not.

Ghost Notes:
The unstressed notes in a groove; dropped notes; nearly inaudible pitched or non-pitched sounds; the opposite of accents.
- Jazz players call the unaccented notes *Ghost Notes*. Every groove has a different pattern of accents and ghosts.

- In many of these pieces, the ghosted subdivisions are not written out. Please fill in the missing subdivisions. I could have written out all the ghosted notes using x note-heads as in Strum Etude 3, but this often makes it more difficult to read. So instead, I've generally opted for simplifying the rhythm to represent just the accents, as this is generally the way grooves are notated. You may see quarter notes or 8th notes but the intention is that you will continue to "play" the subdivision ghost notes in between, filling in the missing ghosts even when they are not written. Unless a slur is written, the idea is to keep your arm moving continuously in a steady strum motion.

About Tempos:

Most of the pieces deliberately have no tempo markings. This is because they can be useful at many different tempos, depending on your ability and approach to the etude—what you want to get out of it.

𝄪 = Ghost Note

╱ = Chop

⌐ = Ghost Chop

○ = Air Strum

Strum Etude 1:
Step By Step

See: Chapter 3, *The Strum Bowing Method*

OK, now that you know all about Groovons and grids, let's have a try at our first groove.

Here's's an easy step by step way to learn new grooves. Later we'll learn these steps as the GPS (Groove Proficiency System) but for now, just power through and hang in there and we'll break it down later.

First, get the groove in your voice. Sing this rhythm. You can say "Dah" or "Bop" or any nonsense syllable you like.

Ex. 1A

Dah dah dah   Dah   dah dah

Now, let's find the Groovon. What is the smallest particle of this groove? What would you play if you were playing a shaker? Air strum sixteenth notes like this:

Ex. 1B

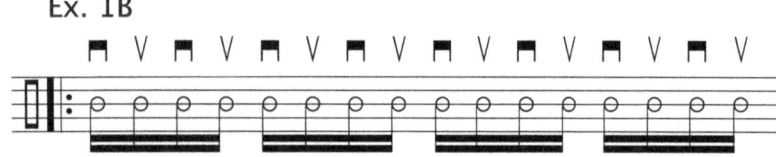

Let's sing the rhythm from Ex. 1A at the same time.

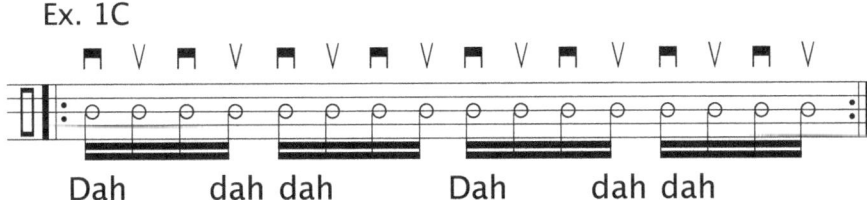

Next, change the lyric from "dah dah dah" to the bow direction lyrics as shown below. Don't stop air strumming!

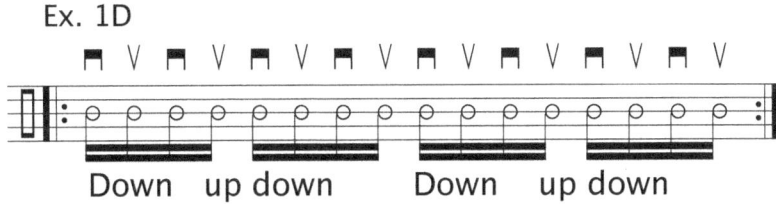

Now, while you air strum and say the bow directions out loud, place your bow on the string, and play the Groovons. Let your voice help you emphasize the accents, but keep your bow moving on all the notes. Make sure you're actually saying, "Down, up down" out loud, not just in your head.

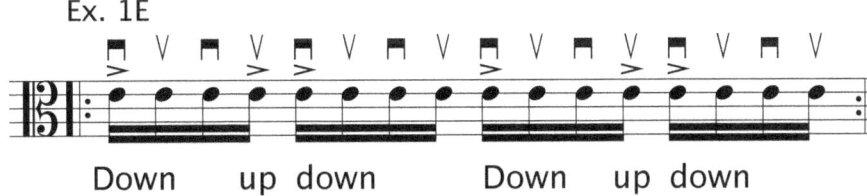

Let's try it again but with a slightly cooler rhythm.

First, get the groove in your voice. Sing this without playing:

Ex. 1F

Dah dah dah dah dah dah dah

Now let's get the groove in our bodies. Air strum the Groovon:

Ex. 1G

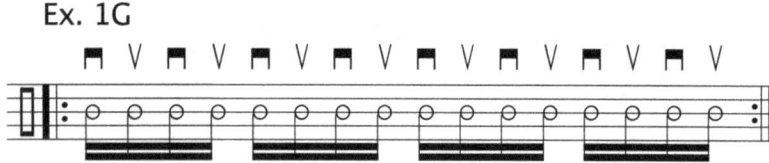

Let's put the two together. While you air strum, add your voice:

Ex. 1H

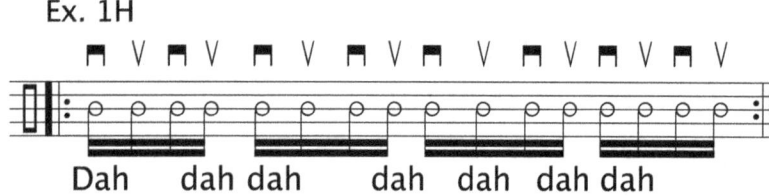

Dah dah dah dah dah dah dah

Next, swap the nonsense lyric for the bow direction lyric, still air strumming.

Ex. 1i

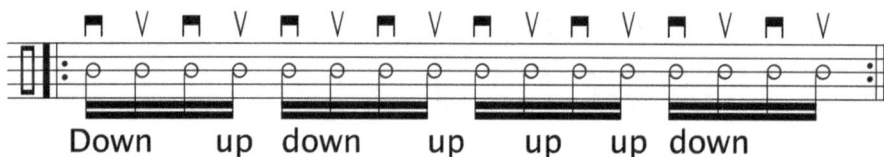

Down up down up up up down

And finally, put the bow on the string and keep singing the bow direction lyric. Let your voice help your bow arm.

Ex. 1J

Down up down up up up down

Groove Prep
Strum Etude: Step By Step

"Step By Step" is a review of what we just worked on. 4 simple steps:

1. **Get the groove in your voice:** Sing the groove
2. **Get the groove in your body:** Air strum the Groovon
3. **Get the groove in your brain:** Say the bow direction. Keep air strumming
4. **Get the groove on your instrument:** Give it a try! Keep singing!

Mike Block (Silk Road Ensemble),
Assoc. Prof., Berklee College of Music
www.mikeblockmusic.com

Strum Etude 1
Step by Step

Tracy Silverman

©2020 From the Gut Music. (ASCAP)

Strum Etude 2:
Shades of the Ghost
Basic Ghosting Skills

See: Chapter 4, *The Strum Bowing Method*

Both hands work together to play ghost notes.

Right hand—tiny bow strokes with minimal bow pressure.
Left hand—dampen the string by either
1) Laying your pinky across the string, or
2) Applying lighter finger pressure.

Dampen

To mute the string by touching it lightly with a finger of the left hand without producing a harmonic.

Let's revisit the exercise from the last chapter and apply these new techniques:

Ex. 2A

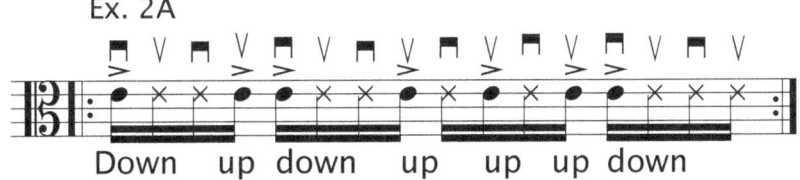

Down   up   down   up   up   up   down

Both hands work together to play ghost notes.

As you play Ex. 2A above, start by playing all the sixteenth notes equally. Then gradually bring out the accents more and more while dropping the ghost notes in between the accents.

Use the chart below to help visualize going from played notes to ghost notes.

When you are ghosting, keep your bow moving back and forth for each sixteenth note. Remember to use tiny bow strokes and to dampen the ghost notes with your left hand.

All notes the same　　　　　　　　　　　　　　　**Accents and ghosts**

Groove Prep
Strum Etude 2: Shades of the Ghost
Basic Ghosting Skills

Start playing all the notes equally in the first bar. Then with each bar, move farther to the right on the shaded diagram above, with the ghost notes getting progressively softer.

Use a combination of **light bow pressure** and **left hand damping** to make your ghost notes as quiet as possible. Use tiny bow strokes. It should almost feel like you're "pinching" the string with the bow on the accents. Then release the pinch for the ghost notes.

Mimi Rabson,
Assoc. Prof., Berklee College of Music
www.mimirabson.com

Strum Etude 2
Shades of the Ghost

Tracy Silverman

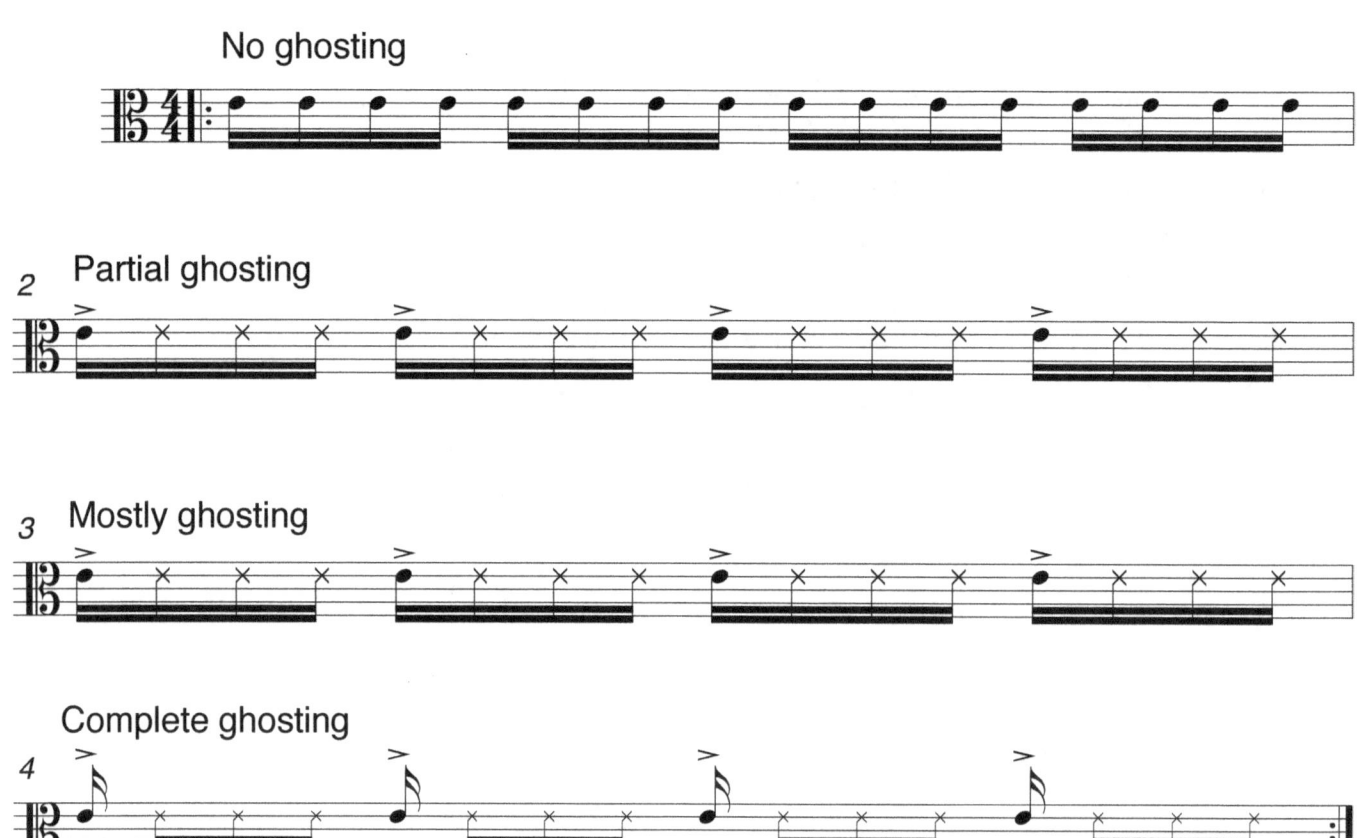

Strum Etude 3:
The Ghost of Grooves Past
Refining Your Ghosting Skills

See: Chapter 4, *The Strum Bowing Method*

Groove Prep
Strum Etude 3: The Ghost of Grooves Past
Refining Your Ghosting Skills

This one is just a little more complicated, requiring a little more control for more accents. Keep working on the pinch and release idea, as you change between accents and ghosts.

Chris Howes
Jazz Violinist, Educator
www.christianhowes.com

Strum Etude 3
The Ghost of Grooves Past

Tracy Silverman

1st time, mute by half-pressing the finger.
2nd time, mute with the 4th finger.
(In bars 9-10 that's the same thing.)

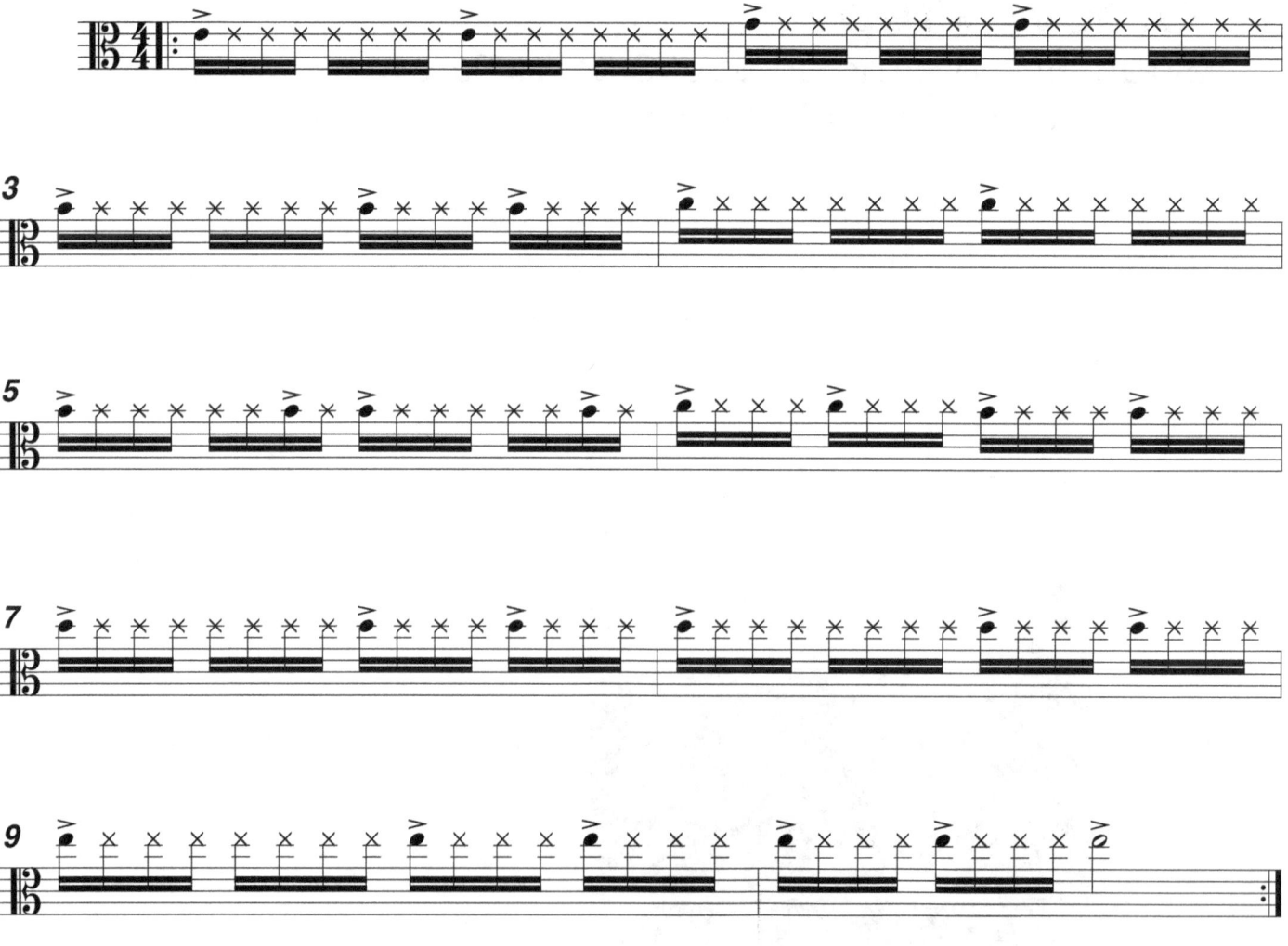

Strum Etude 4:
Groovin' the Ghost
Apply Ghosting to a Groove

See: Chapter 4, *The Strum Bowing Method*

Groove Prep
Strum Etude 4: Groovin' the Ghost
Applying Ghosting to a Groove

This is pretty much the same as Strum Etude 3, but now we are exploring more shades of ghosting. Use the two bars of vocal only at the beginning to get the groove firmly established in your head. Then, keep saying the bow direction while playing because your voice will help you bring out the accents and contrast them with the ghost notes.

Alex DePue
Violinist (Steve Vai)
www.alexdepue.com

Strum Etude 4
Groovin' the Ghost

Tracy Silverman

Strum Etude 5:
Deck the Halls With Placekeeper Notes

See: Chapter 5, *The Strum Bowing Method*

We can think of the ghost notes we just finished working on as placekeeper notes. They are there to keep the pulse steady by keeping the beats evenly spaced. They're like the small marks on a ruler.

> **Placekeeper Notes**
>
> Ghosted subdivisions that fill long notes or rests and keep you properly aligned on the grid.

Your Inner Drummer

If you're creating or contributing to a groove, it's crucial to hear an inner drummer in your imagination. This inner drummer plays all the Groovons, filling all the gaps between the accents of a groove.

Filling in the Blanks

In the following exercises, we will practice filling in any note longer than a sixteenth note—the Groovon—with additional Groovons.

We're going to take this melody:

Ex. 5A

...and turn it into a placekeeper version with the placekeeper notes shown as ghost notes:

Ex. 5B

Strum Etude 5   14

Or we can take this tune:

...and fill in the missing Groovons with ghost notes.

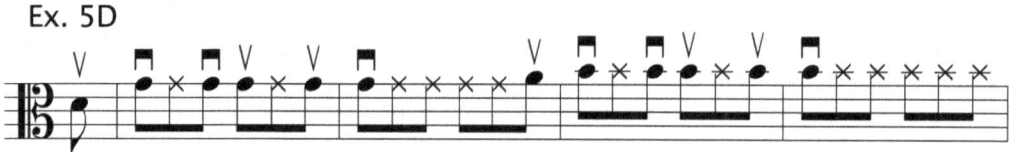

Now that we have our inner drummer playing, let's ghost those placekeepers completely but keep the bowing they created:

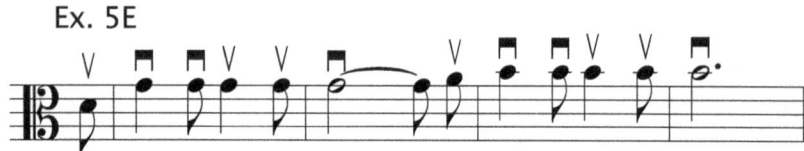

Groove Prep
Strum Etude 5: Deck the Halls with Placekeeper Notes

Remember to use tiny bow strokes at bar 3. At bar 9, play the same as bar 3 but with ghosts so quiet that you barely move the bow at all. Think the placekeepers, but don't actually play them. Feel how your arm wants to move just a little bit to keep the strum going?

Darol Anger
Founding member, Turtle Island String Quartet
Assoc. Prof., Berklee College of Music
www.darolanger.com

Strum Etude 5
Deck the Halls with Placekeeper Notes

Tracy Silverman

Strum Etude 6:
The Groovon in the Dell

See: Chapter 5, *The Strum Bowing Method*

Groove Prep
Strum Etude 6: The Groovon in the Dell

This one is very similar to Strum Etude 5. Start out by ghosting the placekeeper notes. Then, in bar 9, reduce the volume of the ghost notes to zero, but keep the same feeling of the strum in your arm so that the bowing for the accents is the same as when you play all the placekeepers. This will keep the rhythm more precise and help it adhere better to a grid. Notice how the pulse, the strong beats on the first and fourth eighth notes, alternates between down bow and up bow.

Billy Contreras
Jazz Violinist
String Department, Belmont University
www.belmont.edu/music/faculty/faculty_listing_a-g/Contreras_Billy.html

Strum Etude 6
The Groovon in the Dell

Tracy Silverman

©2020 From the Gut Music. (ASCAP)

Strum Etude 7:
Talk to the Hand
The Power of Vocalizing

See: Chapter 6, *The Strum Bowing Method*

You can speed up your learning process just by using your voice.

Tell your arm and hands exactly what you want them to do. "Down up down" is more specific than "Dah dah dah." Your arm may be very skilled, but don't assume it's smart. Give it clear instructions.

If you SAY IT, it will be clearer in your mind and easier to PLAY IT.

If You Can Say It, You Can Play It

Your larynx is located between your brain and your arms. When you say things out loud, your voice makes the connection between your brain and fingers. Coincidence? I don't think so.

If you SAY IT, it will be clearer in your mind and easier to PLAY IT.

Groove Prep
Strum Etude 7: Talk to the Hand

We're going to take the "Groovon in the Dell" melody from Strum Etude 6 and use our voices to help coordinate our bowing. Be ready to sing out loud for this because it doesn't really work if you don't. The 6/8 meter makes the bowing a little trickier and less intuitive. That's why we are using our voices to help us get it straight.

Mark Wood
7-String Electric Violinist, founder of Wood Violins,
Mark Wood Rock Orchestra Camp, Electrify Your Strings
www.markwoodmusic.com

Strum Etude 7
Talk to the Hand

Tracy Silverman

Strum Etude 7

Strum Etude 8:
Dancin' Fool
The Power of Physicalizing

See: Chapter 7, *The Strum Bowing Method*

When I use the term *physicalize*, I mean to unlock your muscles and allow your body to engage freely. It means your body is free and allowed to move the way it's supposed to.

Good rhythm playing is always accompanied by some kind of rhythmic body movement: the "dance" of the groove. Rhythmic music is a by-product of rhythmic movement.

When you are connected to that sense of dance and allow it to guide the way you play, listeners respond by feeling like they want to move, too. When dance inspires music, that music inspires dance. It's a non-vicious cycle.

It's really the only way to keep a groove steady. Just ask a drummer or watch a rhythm guitar player. They're movin' to the groovin'. Isaac Newton's law of inertia states that "a body in motion stays in motion."

That motion keeps it steady. Without it, the pulse is likely to rush or drag.

A great groove sounds like it has always been there, like it started before time began and will never end. Grooves represent infinity. A groove is like a million ton freight train on a flat prairie that's been rolling along at the exact same speed for days. You can't alter it. You just hop on and ride it for a while.

> **Physicalize**
>
> To activate your inner drummer and express the subdivision of the pulse physically as a strum or other motion; to allow your body to respond to a groove with movement; to dance to the groove.

Rhythmic music is a by-product of rhythmic movement.

Groove Prep
Strum Etude 8: Dancin' Fool

Stand up, even you cello players. Say and play this groove, and let yourself dance while you play it. Don't force yourself to move, but focus on the energy of the groove until the music moves your body. Feel free to let your feet tap, your hips sway, your head move, etc. You may have no problem dancing to music without playing an instrument, but it's not always easy to be relaxed and physically loose while operating a string instrument. Don't worry about a good tone or ghosting or perfect intonation right now. Just shout out the lyrics and get your body into the groove.

Grooves represent infinity.

Strum Etude 8
Dancin' Fool

Tracy Silverman

©2020 From the Gut Music. (ASCAP)

Strum Etude 9A:
GPS
(Groove Proficiency System)

See: Chapter 8, *The Strum Bowing Method*

GPS (Groove Proficiency System) for Strings

1. **Hum It** Get It in Your Voice: Vocalize the Groove
2. **Strum It** Get It in Your Body: Find the Groovon
3. **Say It** Get It in Your Brain: Discover the Bow Direction
4. **Play It!** Get It on Your Instrument

1. Hum It
Get It in Your Voice: Vocalize the Groove

Beatbox this groove. Go ahead and turn it into a whole drum kit or electronic drum beat in your imagination.

Ex. 9A

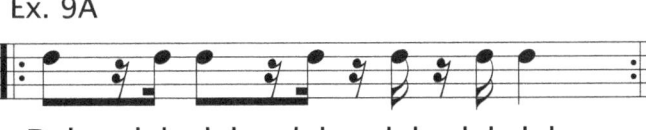

Dah   dah dah   dah   dah dah dah

2. Strum It
Get It in Your Body: Find the Groovon

Next, strum an imaginary guitar. You should be air bowing all of the sixteenth notes, not just the accents. Keep beatboxing!

Ex. 9B

Dah   dah dah   dah   dah   dah dah

Strum Etude 9A   26

3. Say It
Get It in Your Brain: Discover the Bow Direction
Gradually slow down your beatboxing of the groove until you are going slowly enough to be able to verbalize each Groovon. It should sound like this: "DOWN up down UP DOWN up down UP down UP down UP DOWN up down up."

Now drop all the unstressed notes, and what you're left with is the Bowing Key to playing the groove. "DOWN, UP DOWN, UP, UP, UP DOWN." Shout these bow direction lyrics like commands to your bow arm.

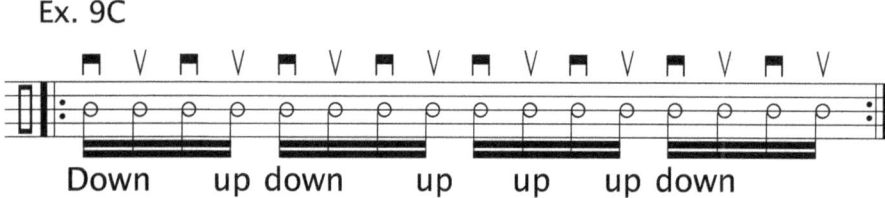

Ex. 9C

Down   up down   up   up   up down

4. Play It!
Get It on Your Instrument
If you can say it, you can play it.

Now, while you're shouting those bow directions, go ahead and put your bow on the strings.

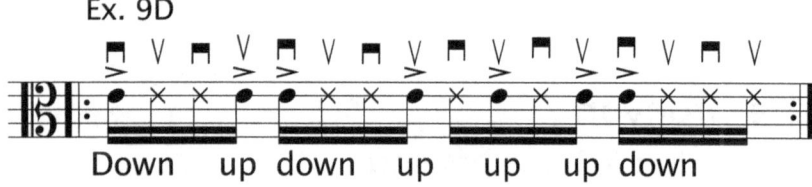

Ex. 9D

Down   up down   up   up   up down

Keep the constant strum going the whole time while you emphasize the accents.
Dial in your ghosting. Remember to use tiny bows and little "pinches" on the accents.

Groove Prep
Strum Etude 9A: GPS (Groove Proficiency System)

1. **Hum It** Get It in Your Voice: Vocalize the Groove
2. **Strum It** Get It in Your Body: Find the Groovon
3. **Say It** Get It in Your Brain: Discover the Bow Direction
4. **Play It!** Get It on Your Instrument

Tracy Silverman and Darol Anger

Strum Etude 9A
GPS: Groove Proficiency System

Tracy Silverman

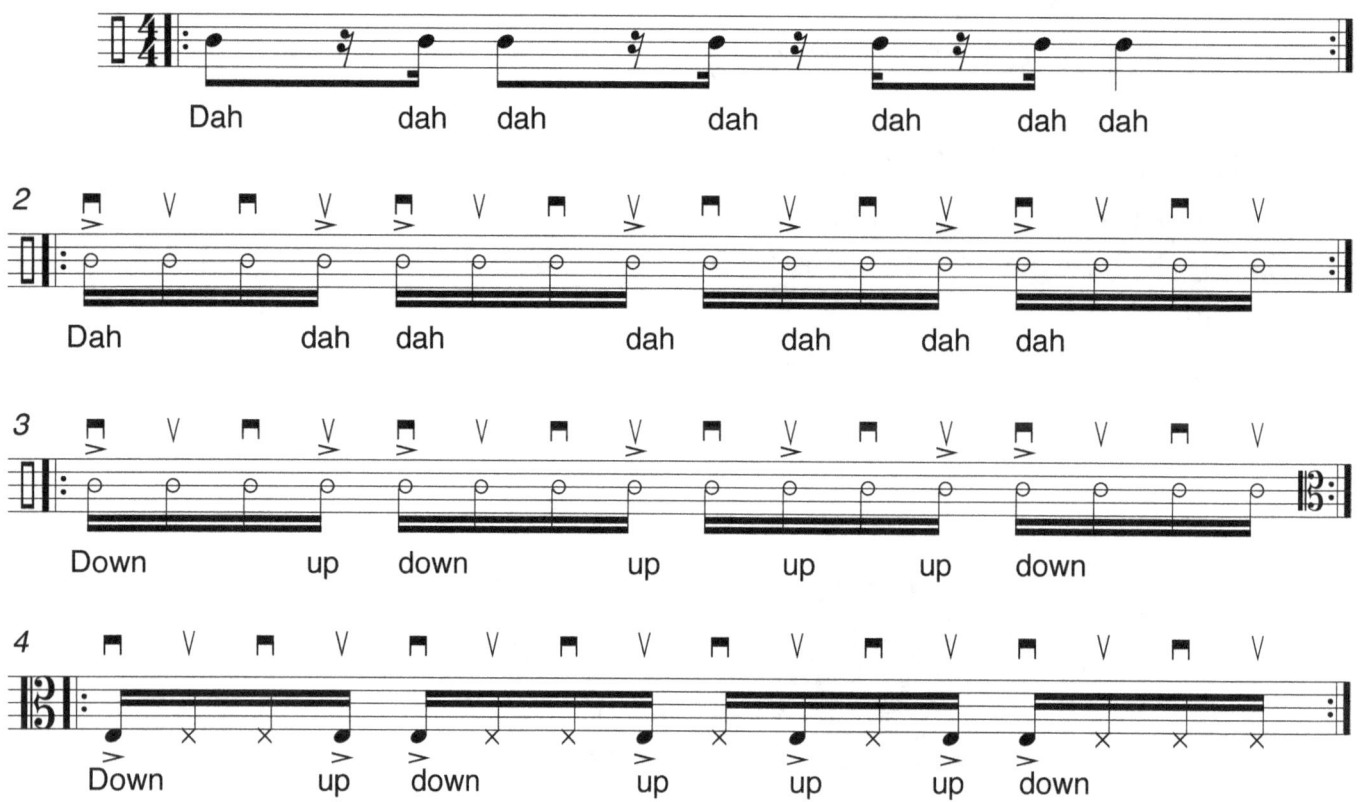

©2020 From the Gut Music. (ASCAP)

Strum Etude 9B:
The Strumming Waubonsies

See: Chapter 8, *The Strum Bowing Method*

Groove Prep
Strum Etude 9B: GPS
The Strumming Waubonsies

This piece explores the fertile area between accents and ghosts. By filling in sustained melody notes with subdivisions, you can choose how played or ghosted you want the melody to be, while still retaining the groove. Also, stay limber with your accents so you can accent all the many syncopations on the up-bow off beats.

Strum Etude 9B
The Strummin' Waubonsies

for Waubonsie Valley High School

Tracy Silverman

Strum Etude 9B
The Strummin' Waubonsies

Strum Etude 10:
Down Down Down!

See: Chapter 9, *The Strum Bowing Method*

Let's learn a new groove using our GPS from Strum Etude 9.

---

1. **Hum It** Get It in Your Voice: Vocalize the Groove
2. **Strum It** Get It in Your Body: Find the Groovon
3. **Say It** Get It in Your Brain: Discover the Bow Direction
4. **Play It!** Get It on Your Instrument

---

1. Hum It
Get It in Your Voice: Vocalize the Groove

Put down your instrument and beatbox this groove. As before, allow your body to move freely and help you get into the groove. You can make drum sounds, or you can say "Dah dah dah" or anything you like. You could say "Bar-Bar-Bar, Bar-be-cue Pork" because the groove sounds a little like "Barbara Ann" by the Beach Boys. (If you're a vegetarian, you can say "Bro-Bro-Bro, Broc-co-li Soup.")

Ex. 10A

Dah dah dah   dah   dah dah dah

2. Strum It
Get It in Your Body: Find the Groovon
While you beatbox, strum an imaginary guitar.

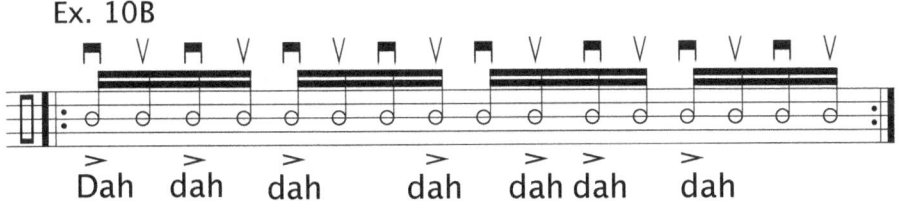

3. Say It
Get It in Your Brain: Discover the Bow Direction
Slow it down and say "Down, up, down, up…" on each Groovon, but maintain the accents from the groove as you do this. It should sound like this: "DOWN up DOWN up DOWN up down UP down UP DOWN up DOWN up down up." This reveals your Bowing Key to this groove as, "DOWN DOWN DOWN, UP, UP DOWN DOWN." These are the commands you need to give to your bow arm as you air bow.

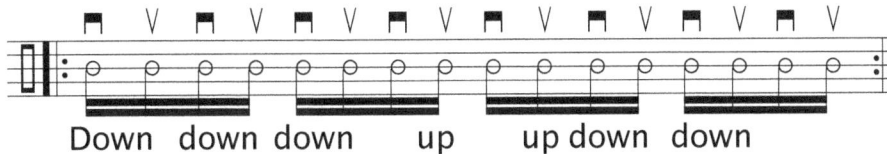

4. Play It!
Get It on Your Instrument
If you can say it, you can play it.

Keep saying the bow direction, and keep air bowing to make sure you have your strum locked in. Put your bow on the strings, and keep it moving in sixteenth notes while your voice helps you bring out the accents: "DOWN DOWN DOWN, UP, UP DOWN DOWN."

Ex. 10D

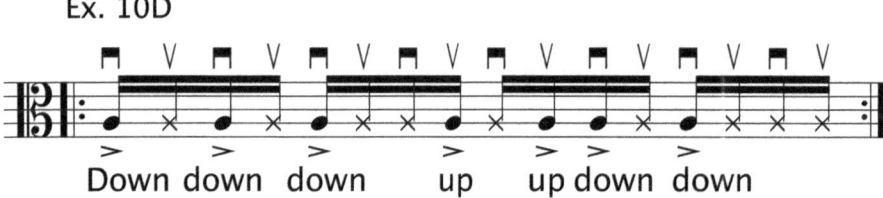

Try to get those ghosts to vanish into thin air. Remember to use tiny bows!

Groove Prep
Strum Etude 10: "Down Down Down!"

Remember that this bowing:

Ex. 10E

...is shorthand for this:

Ex. 10F

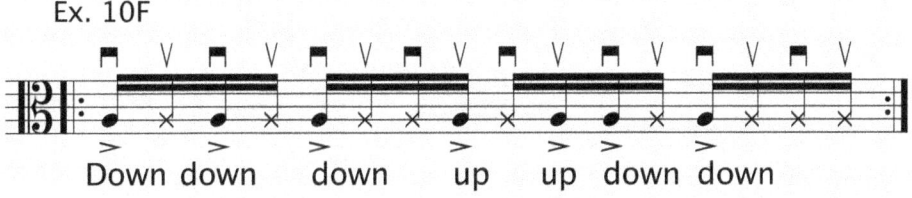

Down down   down   up   up down down

Tracy Silverman and Darol Anger

Strum Etude 10
Down Down Down!

Tracy Silverman

Strum Etude 10

Fill in with ghosted 16th notes notes

Strum Etude 11:
Doin' the Strum

See: Chapter 10, *The Strum Bowing Method*

Let's learn another new groove using our GPS.

1. **Hum It** Get It in Your Voice: Vocalize the Groove
2. **Strum It** Get It in Your Body: Find the Groovon
3. **Say It** Get It in Your Brain: Discover the Bow Direction
4. **Play It!** Get It on Your Instrument

1. Hum It
Get It in Your Voice: Vocalize the Groove
Sing and beatbox the groove in Ex. 11A below. Go ahead and let your body move with the groove.

Ex. 11A

2. Strum It
Get It in Your Body: Find the Groovon
While you're verbalizing the rhythm, air strum the Groovons.

Ex. 11B

3. Say It
Get It in Your Brain: Discover the Bow Direction

Now, call out the bow directions of the accents as you air bow. Slow it down and say "DOWN up DOWN up DOWN up DOWN UP down UP down UP down UP down UP." Then, drop out the unstressed words to reveal your Bowing Key: "DOWN DOWN DOWN DOWN UP UP UP UP UP."

Ex. 11C

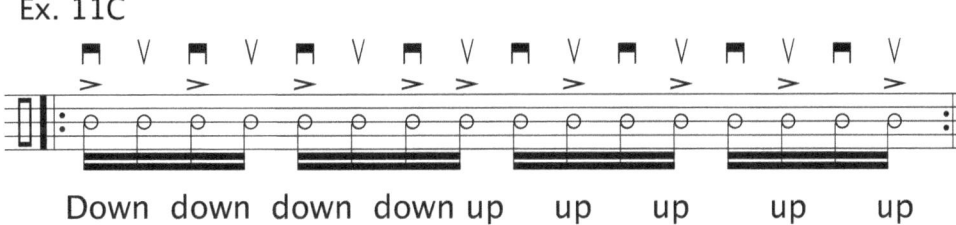

Down   down   down   down   up   up   up   up   up

4. Play It!
Get It on Your Instrument

Now, place your bow on the string, play all of the sixteenth notes, and let your voice direct your arm to emphasize the accents of the groove. Try to ghost those placekeeper notes as much as possible. Remember to use tiny bow strokes and to mute the strings with your left hand when you play the ghost notes

Ex. 11D

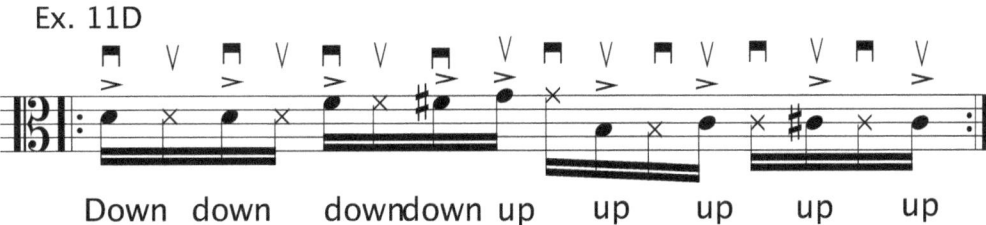

Down   down   downdown up   up   up   up   up

You can apply Strum Bowing to any riff. It's a simple process that never changes: all down beats are down bow and all up beats are up bow. Easy to remember.

Play
Random Tunes

The best way to develop a well-rounded technique is to work in a number of different genres. Just as we are better people when we know and love many different kinds of people, we are better musicians when we know and love many different kinds of music.

Surf a variety of radio stations or Internet playlists, or choose tunes randomly from your music collection. Whatever tune comes up, challenge yourself to break down the learning process with the Groove Proficiency System and figure out how to play it using Strum Bowing

Groove Prep
Strum Etude 11: Doin' the Strum

All the bowings in this piece are consistent with the rule of Strum Bowing: all down beats are down bows, and all up beats are up bows. I've written out some of the ghosted subdivisions (bars 5-6) and not others (bars 3-4), but they should all be very similar gradations of ghosting.

Strum Etude 11
Doin' the Strum

Tracy Silverman

Strum Etude 11

Strum Etude 12:
Variations on a Groove

See: Chapter 11, *The Strum Bowing Method*

Variety

Good rhythm players have an instinct for variety. They understand that the human brain is designed to start ignoring things after a short time if they remain static, so their playing is vibrantly alive and constantly in flux. It breathes with the music. Yes, there is beauty in repetition, but not necessarily in exact repetition.

Yes, there is beauty in repetition, but not necessarily in exact repetition.

Unpredictability

Many rhythm players will keep you involved by intentionally throwing in seemingly random accents. By focusing on the underlying subdivision, the strum, you can shape and spice up your groove without losing it. In fact, it's much easier to do that than to keep playing the same thing over and over again as exactly as possible. That's work. You don't work a cello.

Groove Prep
Strum Etude 12: Variations on a Groove

This Groove Study is more of a guided improvisation. Start with our familiar Practice Groove 1 as your home base. Next, you'll play a variation of it. Then, try to make up your own variations. After that, come back to the original home base groove. Repeat.

David "Doc" Wallace
Chair of the String Dept.,
Berklee College of Music
www.docwallacemusic.com

Strum Etude 12
Variations on a Groove

Tracy Silverman

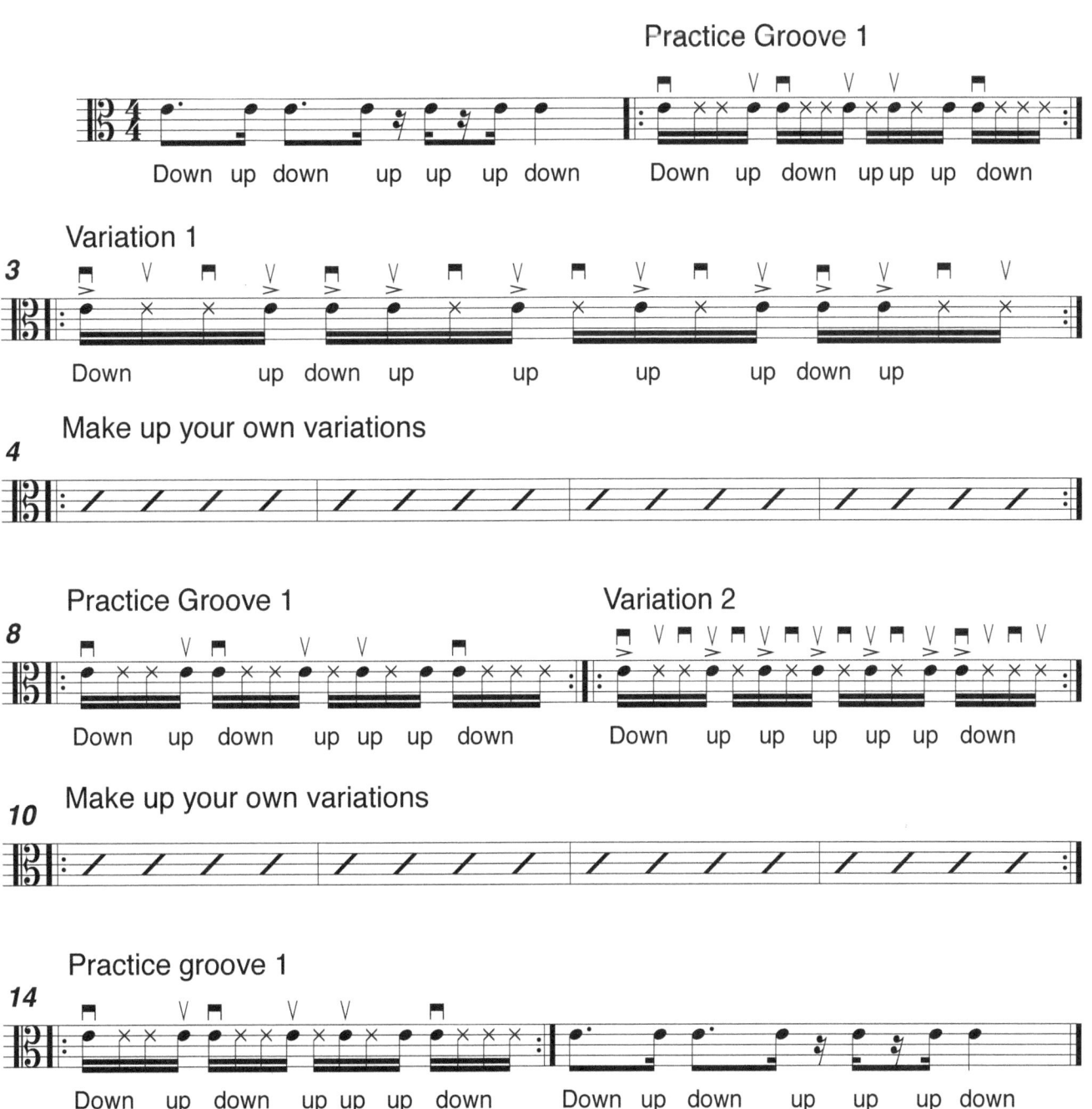

Strum Etude 13A:
Triplets and the 12/8 Shuffle

See: Chapter 12, *The Strum Bowing Method*

The consistent up/down strum that we've been using in the previous Practice Grooves also applies to triplets, quintuplets and other odd numbered groupings or meters.

Some styles, such as Celtic tunes in 6/8 or 9/8 time and 12/8 blues shuffles, subdivide each beat into groups of three. As with any other application of Strum Bowing, the bow maintains consistent down/up subdivisions. But in odd number groupings, the downbeat accents alternate between down and up bows. For instance:

Ex. 13A

As you practice this, try to make the up bow accents equal to the down bow accents. Use your voice to help you.

Groove Prep
Strum Etude 13A: Triplets and the 12/8 Shuffle

This piece is all about getting comfortable with triplet accents. That means getting comfortable with strong up bow accents on the back beat, the second and fourth beats of the bar.

In bar 11, I introduce the idea of repeated down and up bows. Add placekeeper ghost notes in between them so that the idea of the strum from bars 9-10 carries over into bars 11-12.

Bars 25-28 introduce a cross rhythm. This may be a little tricky at first, but it will probably feel natural very quickly. It's a little difficult to read but not hard to play.

Strum Etude 13A
Triplets and the 12/8 Shuffle

Tracy Silverman

Casey Driessen
Program Director, Master of Music in Contemporary Performance,
Berklee College of Music, Valencia
www.caseydriessen.com

Strum Etude 13B:
Magic Sixes

See: Chapter 12, *The Strum Bowing Method*

Groove Prep
Strum Etude 13B: Magic Sixes

The magical part is that six divides into 2 groups of 3 or 3 groups of 2. Depending on how you accent the subdivisions, you can create wonderful cross rhythms.

Strum Etude 13B
Magic Sixes

Tracy Silverman

Strum Etude 13C:
Cross Currents

See: Chapter 12, *The Strum Bowing Method*

Groove Prep
Strum Etude 13C: Cross Currents

This piece works with the idea of 3 against 2 within the context of a 12/8 shuffle.

Strum Etude 13C
Cross Currents

Tracy Silverman

©2020 From the Gut Music. (ASCAP)

Strum Etude 13D:
Groovin' the Seven

See: Chapter 12, *The Strum Bowing Method*

Groove Prep
Strum Etude 13D: Groovin' the Seven

At first it may feel, well, odd to play in 7, but it doesn't take long for it to become muscle memory. In this piece, I've kept it very consistent rhythmic pattern of 2+2+3, first with the accents on downbows and then on upbows. Think about keeping those downbow and upbow accents even in terms of loudness as well as rhythm.

Strum Etude 13D
Groovin' the Seven

Tracy Silverman

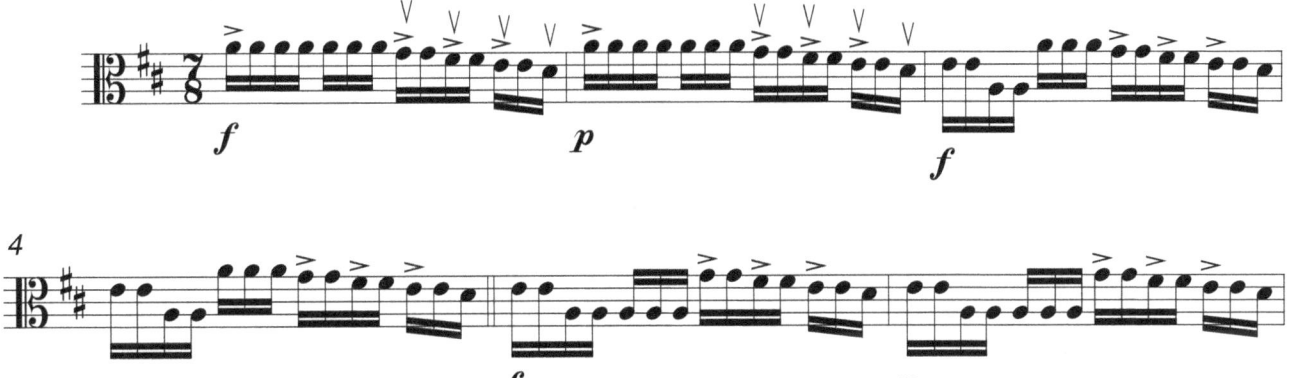

©2020 From the Gut Music. (ASCAP)

Strum Etude 13D

Strum Etude 13E:
Smooth Fiver

See: Chapter 12, *The Strum Bowing Method*

Groove Prep
Strum Etude 13E: Smooth Fiver

Don't rush this one. Let it have a slow lilt and allow your body to move. You can help yourself keep the tempo and groove consistent by allowing the music to move your body in time. Pretty soon, moving and playing in 5 or 7 will feel as natural as 4/4.

Strum Etude 13E
Smooth Fiver

Tracy Silverman

©2020 From the Gut Music. (ASCAP)

Strum Etude 13E

Strum Etude 14:
Chop 'Til You Drop

See: Chapter 13, *The Strum Bowing Method*

The *Chop* is the vertical form of Strum Bowing. It is a non-pitched percussive sound. We can isolate it and use it as a simple back beat, or we can adapt it into a non-pitched version of Strum Bowing, complete with accents and ghosts. Once we develop the Chop, we can combine it with the horizontal Strum Bowing we learned to create something I call a 3D Strum.

It's not a down bow. It's an out bow.

The Down Stroke

For the basic down stroke, you are going to throw the bow onto the string and leave it there. It's not a down bow. It's an *out bow*.

Chuck Bontrager (Tributosaurus)
Concertmaster, Hamilton Chicago Orchestra
www.chuckbontrager.com

Five Rules of The Chop

1. **At the frog** The placement of the stroke is at the very bottom of the bow, as low in the bow as you can get without hitting the metal ferrule at the frog.
2. **Hair out** Rotate the bow so the hair is away from you. This rotation causes the bow to skid away from you a tiny bit when it hits the string. That tiny skid is what produces the chop sound. On violin and viola, that means the stick is toward you and the hair is toward the fingerboard. On cello and bass, the stick is toward you and the hair is toward the bridge.
3. **Right hand loose** Keep your bow grip relaxed and loose so that the bow is free to skid as it hits the strings. Otherwise it won't make much, if any, sound.
4. **Dampen the strings** Dampen the strings with the left hand. (See Ch. 4: "Ghost Notes—How to *Not* Play An Instrument.") Don't push the strings down all the way or you will hear pitched notes.
5. **Leave bow on the strings** After you throw the bow onto the strings, leave it right there. Don't bounce it. This is so you can then make a sound with the up stroke.

As you try out this new stroke, review the five rules above to keep yourself on track.

Ex 14A

What you are shooting for is a completely non-pitched "chuck" that sounds a little bit like a snare drum. Practice for consistency of tone and dynamics. You can Chop on any string you like, and it's often a good idea to land on 2 strings at once so you can throw the bow a little harder.

The Up Stroke

The reason we leave the bow on the string after the chop (rule number five) is so that we can then make a sound when we pick it back up. Pull the bow up off the string with a quick jerking motion with your fingers and wrist so that it catches the string and makes a non-pitched, short percussive noise similar to the noise of the down stroke. It's almost like pizzicato with the bow. Practice this until you can make the up stroke as loud as the down stroke.

I call this basic Chop stroke a Simple Chop. We will learn about the Compound Chop in the next Groove Study.

Ex. 14B

Groove Prep
Strum Etude 14: Chop 'Til You Drop

The first four bars are only down strokes so that you can focus on making sure you are following the Five Rules of the Chop. Don't be concerned if your bow makes a little up stroke sound on the rest as you pick it up for the next down stroke. Then, in bars 5-6 and 9-10, you have the chance to practice the up stroke. Try to make it as loud as the down stroke.

Rachel Barton Pine
Concert Violinist, Recording Artist
rachelbartonpine.com

Strum Etude 14
Chop Till You Drop

Tracy Silverman

©2020 From the Gut Music. (ASCAP)

Strum Etude 15:
Double-time It

See: Chapter 14, *The Strum Bowing Method*

The *Compound Chop* is a double-time version of the Simple Chop.

In order to integrate the Chop into Strum Bowing, we need to be able to play Groovons using the vertical stroke. The Compound Chop allows us to strum vertically just as we learned to strum horizontally.

Ex. 15A

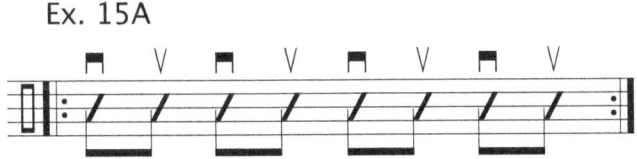

As you play the Simple Chop above, start to play more quietly. Don't throw the bow as hard, don't lift it as far from the strings and economize your motions and bow usage. Gradually, let the tempo get faster. Don't force it; just let it creep faster and faster as the motions become smaller and it gets more comfortable.

Let's think of the rhythm as sixteenths rather than eighths.

Ex. 15B

As you play this sixteenth note chop, add an accent on the first of each group of four Groovons.

Ex. 15C

Power Stroke, Rest Stroke

Let's call that first accent the Power Stroke and the third Groovon the Rest Stroke. In between the Power Stroke and the Rest Stroke are two unaccented placekeeper up strokes that keep us accurately lined up on the grid.

If we zoom in on the microscopic level of one beat, it would look like this:

Ex. 15D

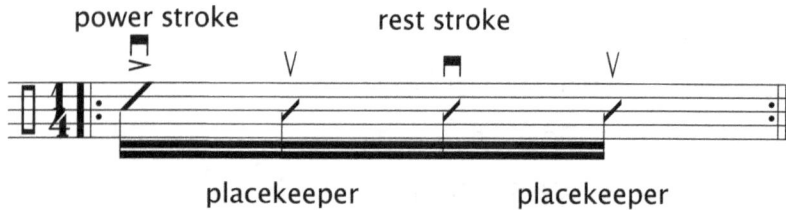

Groove Prep
Strum Etude 15: Double-time It

Keep you motions small and efficient, especially on the faster compound chops.

Martin Hayes
Irish fiddler
(The Gloaming, The Martin Hayes Quartet)

Strum Etude 15
Double-time It

Tracy Silverman

Strum Etude 16:
Hit It on the Back Beat

See: Chapter 14, *The Strum Bowing Method*

The Back Beat

Once you have the Compound Chop under control, you can take it up a notch by adding a Back Beat. All that means is that you put a heavier accent on the second and fourth beats.

Ex. 16A

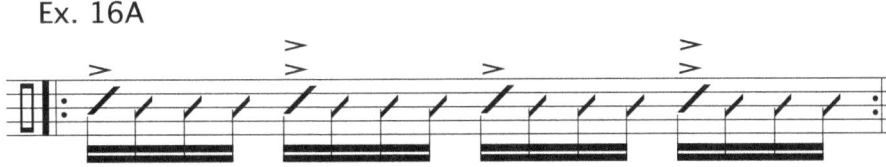

Groove Prep
Strum Etude 16: Hit It on the Back Beat

This piece adds a backbeat to the Chop the Compound Chop. Using your voice to say the bow direction will help. In bar 19, there is a Led Zeppelin-inspired riff. The three down bows imply unwritten ghosted up bows in between. Also there are a few place for you to practice switching quickly from vertical chops to horizontal bow strokes, such as bars 15 and 18.

Strum Etude 16

Everybody Hit It on the Back Beat

Tracy Silverman

©2020 From the Gut Music. (ASCAP)

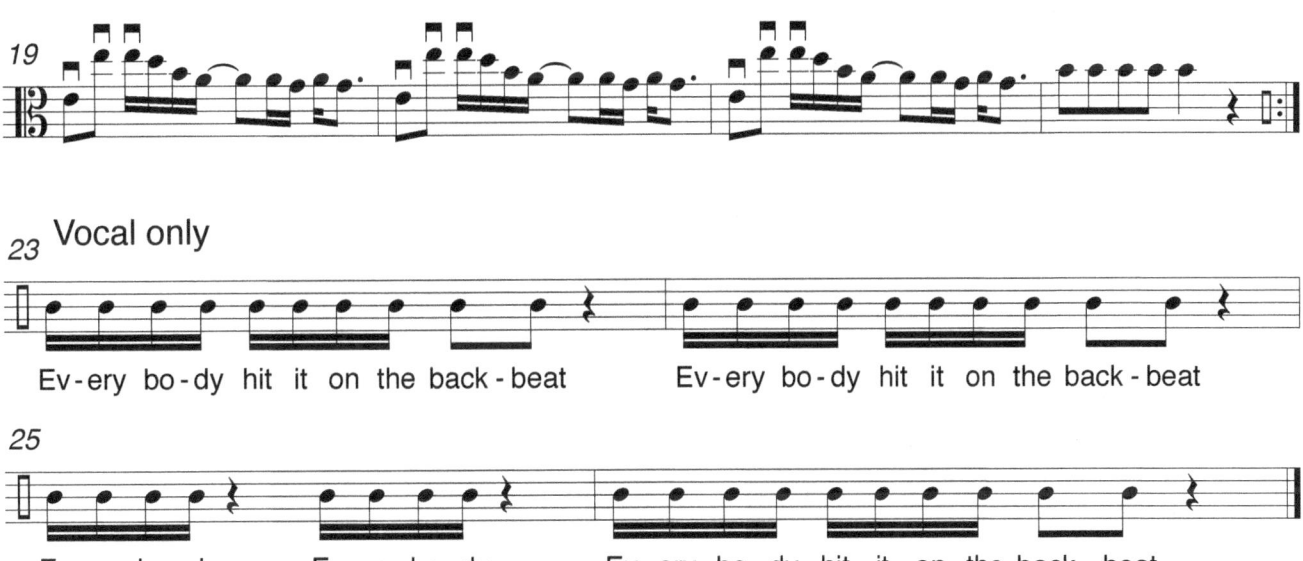

Strum Etude 17A:
Groovin' the Chop

See: Chapter 15, *The Strum Bowing Method*

Let's go back to the 3 practice grooves from Strum Etudes 9, 10 and 11 and see if we can play them with vertical strokes instead of horizontal ones. When we play these grooves with vertical strokes, it doesn't matter what the notes are. We are playing only the rhythm of the groove as if we were playing a non-pitched percussion instrument instead of a violin.

Daniel Bernard Roumain (DBR)
Professor of Practice & Institute Professor
Herberger Institute for Design and the Arts (ASU)
www.danielroumain.com

Practice Groove 1

Here is Practice Groove 1 from Strum Etude 9A:

Ex. 17A

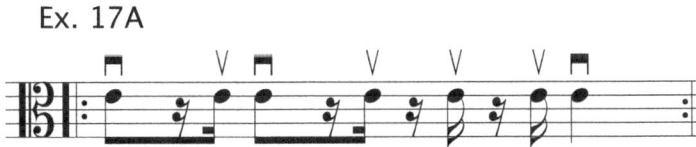

Here is how we actually play it with the added placekeeper ghost notes:

Ex. 17B

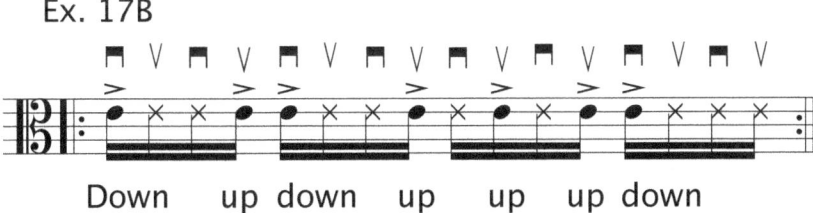

Down   up down   up   up   up down

To play this same groove as a vertical chop, start by playing a Compound Chop.

Ex. 17C

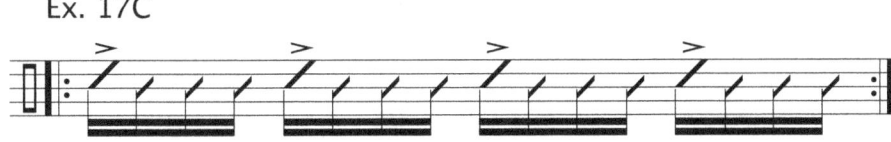

Now, add the accents of Practice Groove 1. Use your voice to help.

Ex. 17D

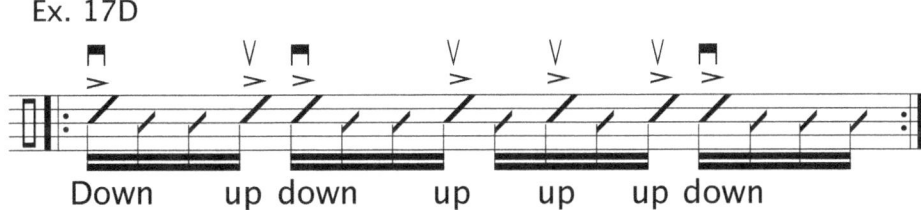

Down   up down   up   up   up down

Practice Groove 2

Let's apply this same process to Practice Groove 2 from Strum Etude 10. Here's the shorthand version:

Ex. 17E

...which we actually play like this with added placekeeper notes:

Ex. 17F

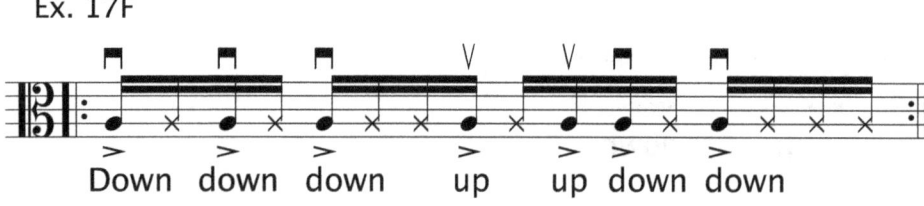

...and which can be played vertically like this:

Ex. 17G

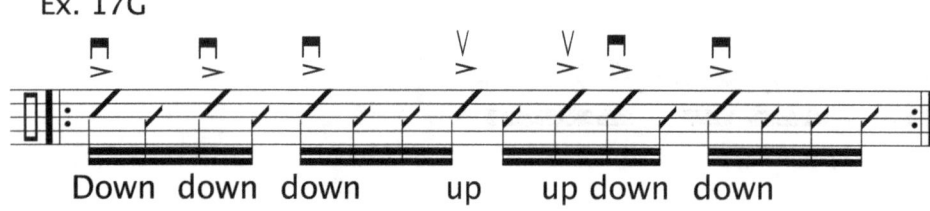

Practice Groove 3

Here's Practice Groove 3 from Strum Etude 11:

Ex. 17H

Here it is with the ghosted placekeeper notes:

Ex. 17i

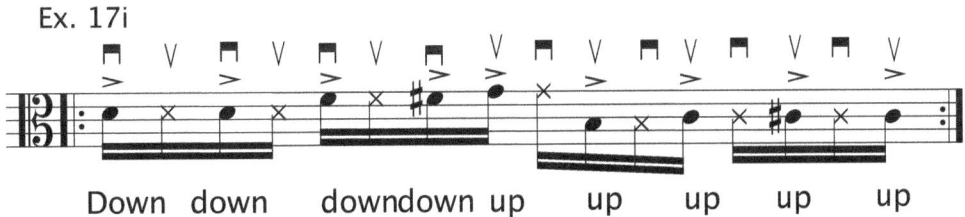

Down down   downdown up   up   up   up   up

And here it is as a vertical Chop pattern:

Ex. 17J

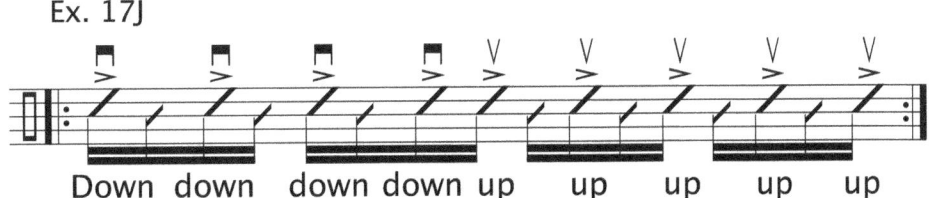

Down down   down down up   up   up   up   up

Groove Prep
Strum Etude 17A: Groovin' the Chop

We start by reviewing our Simple and Compound Chops. Then, we take the practice grooves we learned horizontally in Strum Etudes 1, 9, 10 and 11 and play them vertically. As always, use your voice to help you play the rhythms.

The Turtle Island String Quartet
circa 1995

Strum Etude 17A
Groovin' the Chop

Tracy Silverman

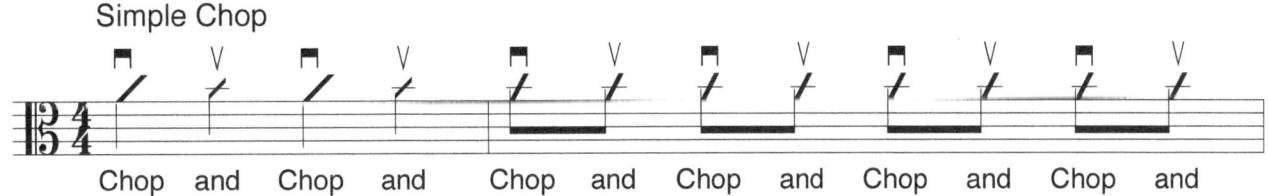
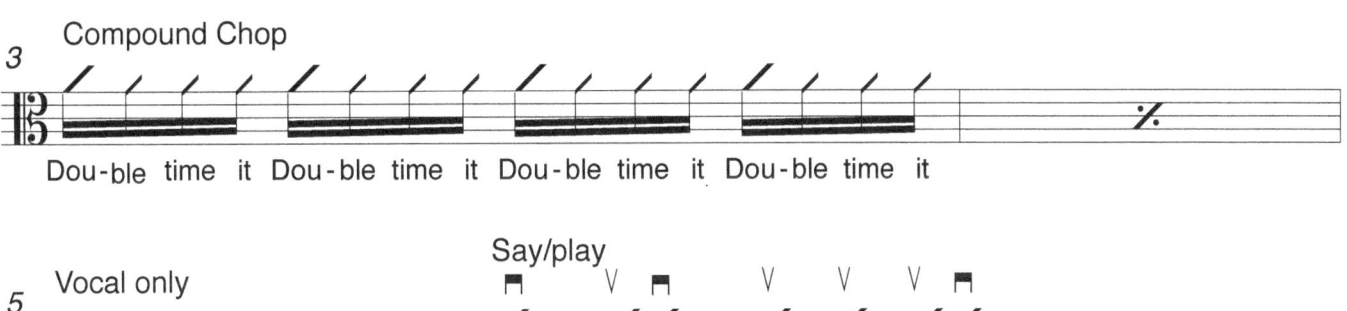
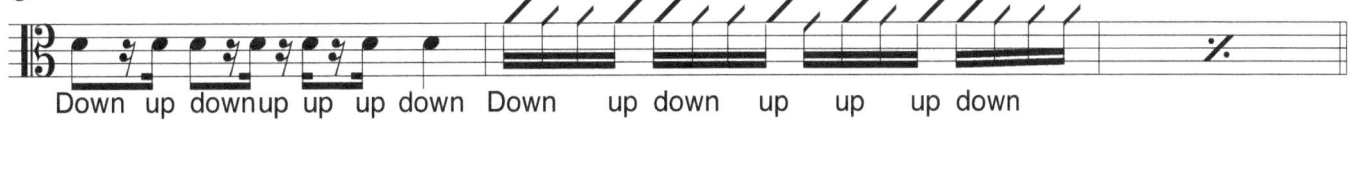
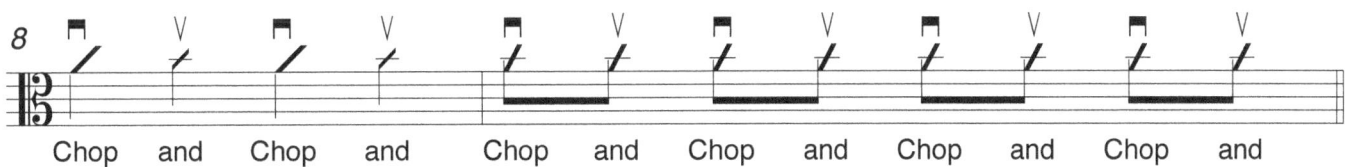

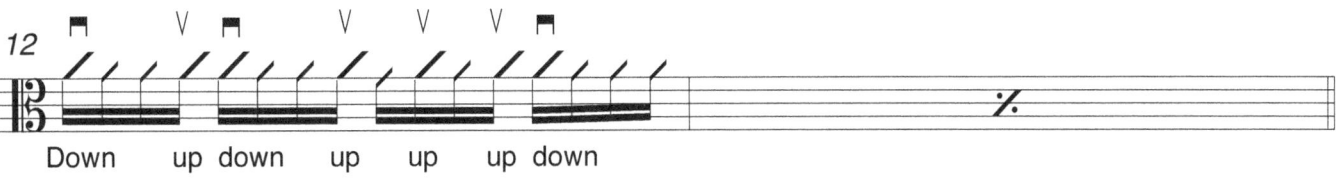
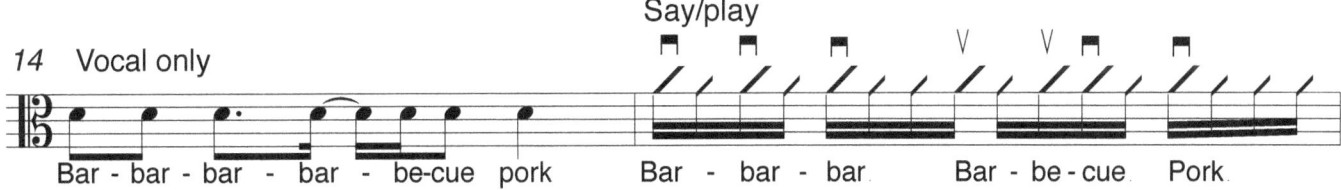

©2020 From the Gut Music. (ASCAP)

Strum Etude 17B:
Swingin' the Chop

See: Chapter 15, *The Strum Bowing Method*

Groove Prep
Strum Etude 17B: Swingin' the Chop

If you allow your basic strum to be a little lopsided, you will get that swing feel that makes hip-hop sound like hip-hop and jazz sound like jazz. You can control the amount of swing and it's a good idea to get comfortable with changing the amount of swing from more even notes to a fully swung triplet feel.

Strum Etude 17B
Swingin' the Chop

Tracy Silverman

©2020 From the Gut Music. (ASCAP)   Strum Etude 17B   80

Strum Etude 18A:
Changing Gears

See: Chapter 16, *The Strum Bowing Method*

You've mastered horizontal and vertical strokes! Now, you're ready to combine the two.

First, play a Simple Chop.

Ex. 18A

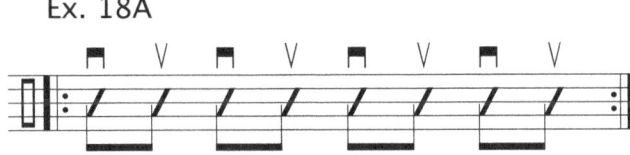

Now, add a horizontal stroke on the first beat.

Ex. 18B

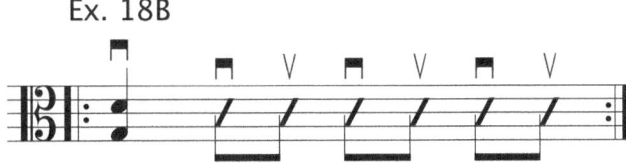

Since the Chop takes place exclusively at the frog, you will play the horizontal notes at the frog as well. Remember to dampen the strings with your left hand for the Chops but to lift the dampening fingers for the horizontal down beat stroke.

Now, double time the Simple Chop to make it a Compound Chop.

Ex. 18C

Add a horizontal note on the downbeat, just as before. And you can also start to bring out the back beat on the second and fourth beats.

Ex. 18D

Now, instead of one horizontal eighth note on the down beat, play two eighth notes.

Ex. 18E

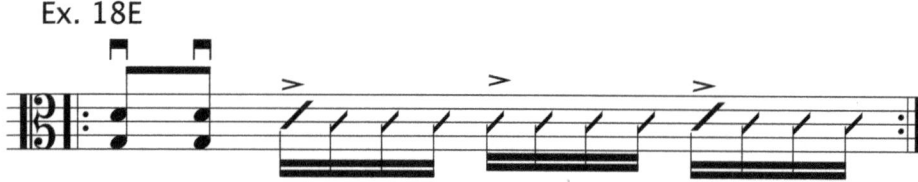

Groove Prep
Strum Etude 18A: Changing Gears

We start with the Simple Chop, then add a horizontal down beat stroke. Then we do the same with the Compound Chop. In bar 11, we add a second horizontal note.

Joe Deninzon,
Electric Violinist, (Stratospheerius)
www.joedeninzon.com

Strum Etude 18A
Changing Gears

Tracy Silverman

Chop and Chop and Chop and Chop and Down Chop and Chop and Chop and

Dou - ble time it Dou - ble time it Dou - ble time it Dou - ble time it

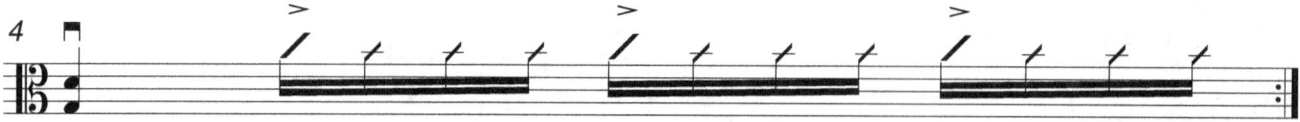
Down   Dou - ble time it Dou - ble time it Dou - ble time it

Down   Dou-ble time it Dou-ble time it Dou-ble time it

Down down Dou-ble time it Dou-ble time it Dou-ble time it

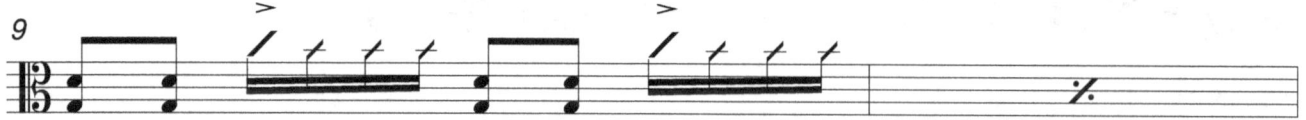
Down down Dou-ble time it Down down Dou-ble time it

Down down Chop Down down Dou-ble time it   Yeah!

©2020 From the Gut Music. (ASCAP)

Strum Etude 18B: Automatic Transmission– Swingin' the Chop 2

See: Chapter 16, *The Strum Bowing Method*

Groove Prep

Strum Etude 18B: Automatic Transmission– Swingin' the Chop 2

Take your time and sink into the funk. If you let it get slow enough, it turns into a 12/8 shuffle feel.

Strum Etude 18B

Automatic Transmission--Swingin' the Chop 2

Tracy Silverman

©2020 From the Gut Music. (ASCAP)

Strum Etude 19A:
3-D Barbecue

See: Chapter 17, *The Strum Bowing Method*

You've just finished learning the basics of the 3-D Strum, a groove that combines vertical and horizontal bow strokes. Let's practice it with some grooves we are already familiar with.

Earl Maneein
Violin, (SEVEN)SUNS, Black Heart Sutra)
www.earlmaneeinmusic.com

Practice Groove 1

We took our Practice Groove 1

...and learned how to play it vertically like this:

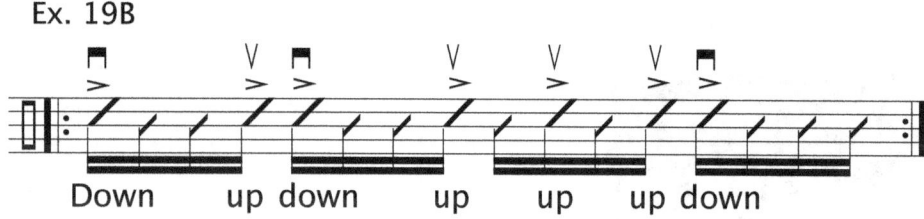

Now let's turn those vertical accents back into horizontal notes. Remember to play it all at the frog.

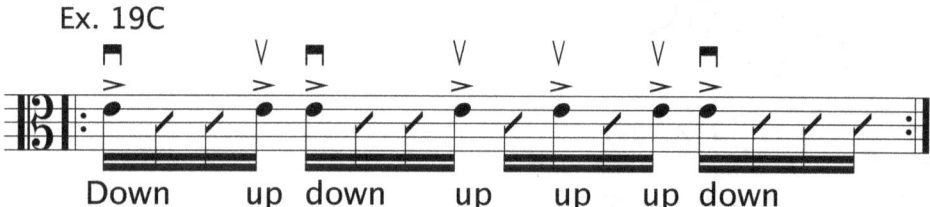

You can take this groove one step further by putting a heavy Chop back beat on the second and fourth beats. Use your left hand to dampen the strings for the vertical Chops but open the strings up to ring on the horizontal strokes. Slow it down if you need to. Use your voice to help you. If you can say it, you can play it!

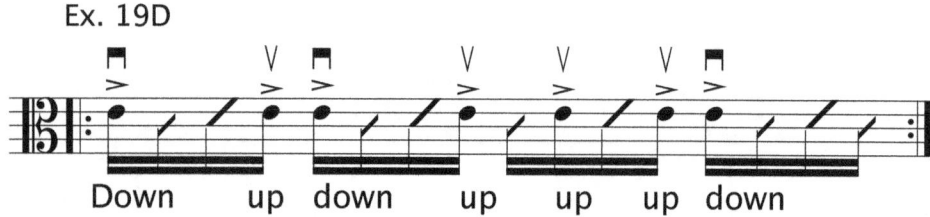

Practice Groove 2

Now let's do the same process for Practice Groove 2 from Chapter 9.

Here's the original riff:

Ex. 19E

Now play the groove vertically like this:

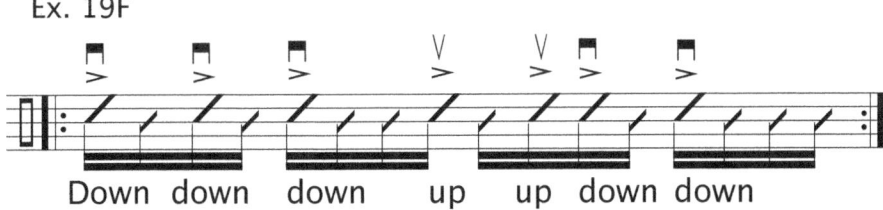

Ex. 19F

Down down down   up   up down down

Let's turn those accents into horizontal bass notes. Remember to keep it all at the frog.

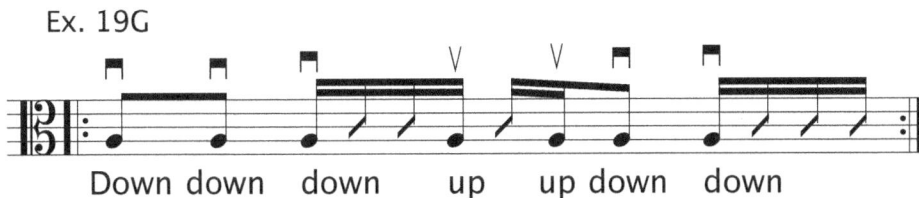

Ex. 19G

Down down down   up   up down down

Now let's replace the bass notes on the backbeats with heavy Chops.

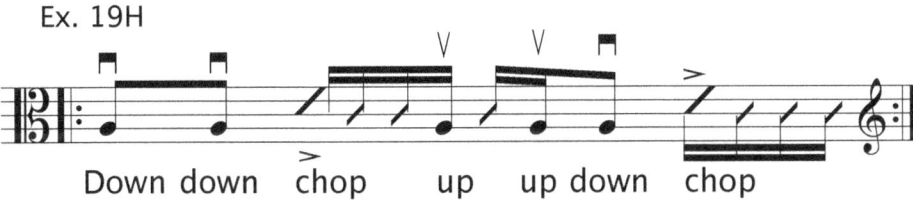

Ex. 19H

Down down chop   up   up down chop

Groove Prep
Strum Etude 19A: 3-D Barbecue

This piece is based on Practice Groove 2. It starts with the 3-D version but in bar 9, we go back to the original groove which you should beatbox with your voice, just to reinforce it. Bars 11-14 could be repeated as a rhythm for someone else to solo on top. The chords would be G7 and C7.

Richard Greene
Violinist, legendary "Inventor of the Chop"
www.richardgreene.net

Strum Etude 19A
3D Barbecue

Tracy Silverman

©2020 From the Gut Music. (ASCAP)

Strum Etude 19B:
Compound Interest

See: Chapter 17, *The Strum Bowing Method*

Groove Prep
Strum Etude 19B: Compound Interest

The focus here is on the compound chop as the default template underlaying so many 3-D strums. Get comfortable with all the up-bow syncopations. Get comfortable with the switch from horizontal downbeat to vertical chops.

Feel free to use this and all the other etudes as leaping-off points for your own improvisations, even if your improvisations are only subtle changes to the original. The feeling of true freedom is often subtle and expressed very economically, without demonstrating tons of freedom and proficiency in terms of improvised notes, rhythms or "fanciness" of one kind or another. For rhythm players, keeping a great pocket is a matter of understatement and support, being responsive to the soloist or vocalist, and knowing how to make the overall musical team stronger than any one player on it.

Strum Etude 19B
Compound Interest

Tracy Silverman

Strum Etude 19

Strum Etude 20:
Groovin' on the Vertizontal

See: Chapter 18, *The Strum Bowing Method*

Groove Prep
Strum Etude 20: Groovin' on the Vertizontal

In this piece, we take 3-D Strum versions of Practice Grooves 1 and 2 and use them in the context of a bass line and melody—the musical equivalent of defining a word by using it in a sentence. At bar 5, we have the harmonized version of the groove with a double-time back beat. In bar 17, we shift to Practice Groove 2, but we start it more minimally, with just a few of the accents, and let it build into the fully accented groove, which doesn't become complete until bar 23. We return to the first groove at bar 27 and end with the riff from bar 12.

Strum Etude 20
Groovin' on the Vertizontal

Tracy Silverman

©2020 From the Gut Music. (ASCAP)

Strum Etude 21:
Freestylin'—A Groove Jam

See: Chapter 19, *The Strum Bowing Method*

The beauty of the Chop and percussive bowing is that there are no pitches to worry about. You can practically ignore your left hand! Rhythmic variation is a great way to get started with improvisation. You'd be surprised how much you can do with just two or three different notes if the rhythms are interesting.

You'd be surprised how much you can do with just two or three different notes if the rhythms are interesting.

Improv Tips

- **Don't disturb the groove.** Listen to what's going on around you, and try to fit in. Be a percussion player. Find the accents of the groove, and Chop along with it.
- **Find the most important pitches being used.** Sing them.
- **Play the pitches that you're singing on your instrument.** Ghost the notes until you're sure about them.
- **Drift higher in the bow** toward the middle; less vertical, more horizontal strokes.
- **Explore. Be flexible.**
- **Move or dance while you play.**
- **Sing along!**

Groove Prep
Strum Etude 21: Freestylin'— A Groove Jam

A quick reference to the Suzuki method in bar 2, and then a highly syncopated riff in bar 4. Bar 15 begins something new. In this section, I have written out all the pitches, but you should supply your own rhythmic groove using accents and ghosts. You could start with one of the two rhythms from earlier in the piece, or you could start with one of the Practice Grooves. I encourage you to venture off into your own territory, using the given pitches as the Groovons. This is a chance for you to improvise a groove!

Julie Lyonn Lieberman
Performer/Author/Educator, Artistic Director: Strings Without Boundaries
www.julielyonn.com

Strum Etude 21
Freestylin': A Groove Jam

Tracy Silverman

Strum Etude 21

FREESTYLE!
Make up your own grooves with 16th notes as the subdivision.
Using any of the notes given, create your own accents and ghosts using vertical, horizontal or 3D strums. Find someone to play the chords or program them into an app like Band in a Box.

Glossary

3-D Strum: A combination of horizontal and vertical strumming.

Back Beat: The second and fourth beats in a 4/4 meter.

Bowing Key: The bow directions determined by Strum Bowing; the bowing that results when you add placekeeper notes to a phrase and impose a constant down/up bowing grid, then remove the placekeepers but retain the bowing.

Chop: Also referred to as the Simple Chop; a non-pitched vertical bow stroke consisting of a down stroke and an audible up stroke.

Compound Chop: A double-time version of the Simple Chop in which the first note is stressed and the other 3 are not.

Dampen: To mute the string by touching it lightly with a finger of the left hand without producing a harmonic.

Feel: The personality that you bring to a groove; those subtle intangibles of timing and dynamics that create a rhythmic character.

Gesture Bowing: Emphasizing with your bow arm the way you might if you were speaking emphatically.

Ghost Notes: The unstressed notes in a groove; dropped notes; nearly inaudible pitched or non-pitched sounds; the opposite of accents.

GPS for Strings: A method for learning how to play new grooves with Strum Bowing. The four steps are:
1. Hum It—Get It in Your Voice: Vocalize the Groove
2. Strum It—Get It in Your Body: Find the Groovon
3. Say It—Get It in Your Brain: Discover the Bow Direction
4. Play It!—Get It on Your Instrument

Grid: A consistent framework that helps keep rhythms evenly aligned; a rhythm ruler; a.k.a. The Groovon Grid.

Groove: A consistent subdivision of the pulse defined by a pattern of accented and ghosted notes.

Groovon: The smallest particle of a rhythmic groove; the smallest usable subdivision of the beat; a Groovon is to a beat what protons and neutrons are to atoms.

Physicalize: To actualize your inner drummer, i.e. to express the subdivision physically as a strum or other motion; to allow your body to respond to a groove with movement; to dance to the groove.

Placekeeper Notes: Ghosted subdivisions that fill long notes or rests and keep you properly aligned on the grid.

Pocket: Another word for groove or feel. Drummers and bass players often refer to being in the pocket or having a great pocket.

Power Stroke: The first, heaviest stroke of the Compound Chop.

Pulse: The beat. For instance, in 4/4 time, there are four pulses per measure.

Rest Stroke: The third, unstressed stroke of the Compound Chop.

Strum Bowing: Using your bow like you're strumming a guitar.

Subdivision: 1) The act of dividing a pulse evenly into smaller increments. For instance, a quarter note can be divided into four sixteenth notes.
2) A fraction of a pulse.

Swing: The unequal subdivision of a pulse, in which the first note is typically twice as long as the second, creating a triplet. The amount of swing can vary from a subtle unevenness to a "hard" swing.

Syncopation: Accenting a normally unaccented up beat. It usually has the feeling of anticipating the following beat.

photo: Eric England

For video and audio demonstrations of the musical examples in this book, audio recordings of the 22 Groove Studies for Strings, and all things Strum Bowing related, please visit **Strumbowing.com**

If you have questions, thoughts or suggestions, please visit and feel free to contact me at **www.tracysilverman.com** where you can also sign up for my newsletter, The Scuttlebutt.

I teach jazz and electric violin at Belmont University in Nashville, TN. For information about workshops/clinics/residencies, teacher training, video lessons or performances, you can reach me at **info@tracysilverman.com**

Visit me at:
Facebook: facebook.com/TracySilvermanMusic
Twitter: @tracysilverman
Instagram: @tracysilverman
Spotify: fanlink.to/spotify-TS
YouTube: youtube.com/tracysilverman

Grooooooooove on....

www.ingramcontent.com/pod-product-compliance
Lightning Source LLC
Chambersburg PA
CBHW081232080526
44587CB00022B/3917